SECRETS

OF AMERICAN HISTORY

★ REVOLUTIONARY WAR ★

No Longer Property of Anythink Libraries / Rangeview Library District

The Founding Fathers Were Spies!

by Patricia Lakin

illustrated by Valerio Fabbretti

Ready-to-Read

Simon Spotlight
New York   London   Toronto   Sydney   New Delhi

SIMON SPOTLIGHT
An imprint of Simon & Schuster Children's Publishing Division
1230 Avenue of the Americas, New York, New York 10020
This Simon Spotlight edition July 2017
Text copyright © 2017 by Simon & Schuster, Inc.
Illustrations copyright © 2017 by Valerio Fabbretti
All rights reserved, including the right of reproduction in whole or in part in any form.
SIMON SPOTLIGHT, READY-TO-READ, and colophon are registered trademarks of Simon & Schuster, Inc.
For information about special discounts for bulk purchases, please contact Simon & Schuster Special Sales at
1-866-506-1949 or business@simonandschuster.com.
Manufactured in the United States of America 0517 LAK
2 4 6 8 10 9 7 5 3 1
This book has been cataloged with the Library of Congress.
ISBN 978-1-4814-9970-5 (hc)
ISBN 978-1-4814-9969-9 (pbk)
ISBN 978-1-4814-9971-2 (eBook)

Contents

Chapter I
Spy in Chief:
George Washington

You might know that George Washington was the first president of the United States, but did you know that he was also a spy? It's true! And he wasn't the only one. Founding fathers like Benjamin Franklin, Alexander Hamilton, and Thomas Jefferson were spies too. So were many other brave women and men in colonial America! To understand why, let's go back in time and unlock the secrets of American history!

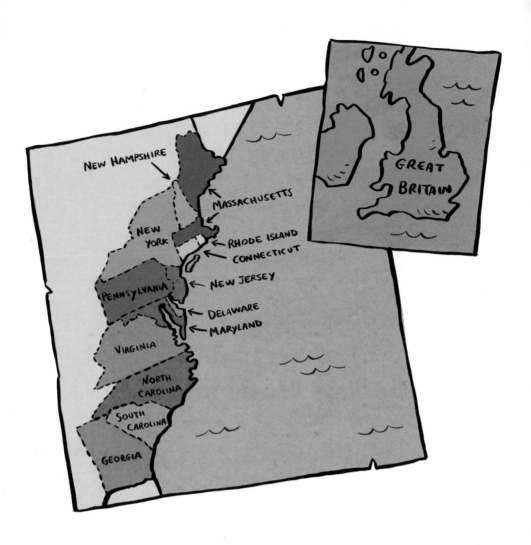

Imagine it's 1774, and you live in one of the thirteen American colonies ruled by King George of Great Britain. His strict laws have made life very hard for you, and you have no way to change them since American colonists are not allowed to be a part of the British Parliament.

You want to rebel against the king and form a new country, but if you speak your mind you could be in big trouble! Colonists who think the way you do are called Patriots. Colonists who are loyal to the king are called Tories, or Loyalists.

That's how it was for years, until a group of Patriots held a meeting in Philadelphia, Pennsylvania, called the First Continental Congress, and invited people from each of the colonies. They wrote to the king to ask for representation but were ignored. Because the king refused to make changes, the Revolutionary War began in 1775. When the Second Continental Congress met that year, Patriots selected George Washington to be the commander of their military, called the Continental army. His mission

was to defeat the British and establish a new country that would be free to make its own rules and laws!

But the Continental army lacked training and equipment compared to the strong British army, so the Patriots' chances of winning the war seemed slim. George Washington realized that the Patriots might be able to win, however, if they were *sneakier* than the British. To do that, they needed to find out information like when and where the British would attack, where they stored supplies, and more. That's where spies came in!

George Washington created a network
of spies called the Secret Committee.
He also created a Committee of Secret
Correspondence . . . but more on *that* later!

Just like modern spies, George
Washington's spies used code names,
disguises, and other techniques to gather
information, which spies call "intelligence."
Soon many colonists were spying on the
British!

In 1777 a woman in Philadelphia named Lydia Darragh didn't have to go far to spy. The British had forced her to let them meet in her home, even though she didn't believe in their cause.

Darragh listened in on their conversations from inside a closet and overheard them planning a surprise attack in a nearby town called Whitemarsh. Legend has it that she pretended she needed to leave to get flour, and she warned the Continental army about the attack!

She also found a clever way to send less urgent information without making her houseguests suspicious. She wrote it on little pieces of paper that she wrapped around buttons! Then she covered the buttons with fabric and sewed them onto a shirt. Her son John would wear the shirt on visits to her older son, Charles, who was in the Continental army. Charles gave the buttons to his commander, who took them apart to read the secret messages inside. Her actions as a spy likely saved many lives!

Chapter 2
Secret Messages

During the Revolutionary War, spies found all kinds of ways to send secret messages. Why did they need to be so secretive? We're glad you asked!

Nowadays if you want to send a message to someone far away, you can call, e-mail, or send a text message. Back then the only option was to send a paper letter delivered by hand, ship, or a courier on horseback.

Soon British spies began to "intercept" the Patriots' mail. This means they read people's letters before delivering them in hopes of finding out important information about the Continental army's plans.

One letter they took was about George Washington's teeth! He had asked his dentist to send supplies so he could clean his teeth himself, since he was with the troops. That might not *sound* very useful, but it may have helped the British learn George Washington's location, since it said he was in New Windsor, New York!

George Washington and his spies began to perform "counterintelligence" missions to keep the British from learning the Continental army's secrets. One way they did this was by spreading false information intended to confuse or mislead the British.

George Washington even wrote fake letters that he *wanted* the British to capture. In one letter he claimed he had far more troops and supplies than he actually had, possibly to seem like more of a threat. The British believed the statements because they recognized George Washington's handwriting!

George Washington and his spies also found ways to deliver messages that were harder to intercept.

Sometimes they used what is called a "dead drop." A spy would place a secret message in a set hiding spot, like a particular hollow tree. Then another spy would come by and pick up the note before anyone saw it!

Other times they hid messages inside regular-looking items, like Lydia Darragh's cloth buttons. Spies also wore shoes with secret compartments inside the heels!

They also sent secret messages to foreign countries to convince the leaders to send money or supplies. That was the mission of George Washington's Committee of Secret Correspondence. And it was led by Benjamin Franklin! He was perfect for the job. He was a respected writer and had friends in Europe, since he had lived there before the American Revolution.

France had recently lost a war to the British, and Benjamin Franklin wondered if they might side with the Patriots.

He secretly wrote to his friends in Spain, France, and other countries. France was willing to help, but *only* if they could be sure the Patriots could win the war. The French sent a secret agent to America to meet with Benjamin Franklin to get more information, but Benjamin Franklin thought he might be a "double agent" for the British. A double agent is someone who is pretending to be loyal to one group or country but is actually spying for another group or country.

Benjamin Franklin's friend John Jay was experienced in investigating double agents and agreed to attend the meetings to help make sure the Frenchman could be trusted. Even so, each night they met, a cautious Benjamin Franklin took a different route from his home to Carpenter's Hall in Philadelphia. Then he closed all the shutters so nobody would see them meeting. They decided that the Frenchman wasn't a double agent, but the Continental army still needed to prove that they could win.

To do that, Benjamin Franklin wrote a glowing report about the Continental army, saying that it was large, well-supplied, and highly successful . . . even though that wasn't the case. It worked. France sent supplies and funds that helped win the war!

Chapter 3
Invisible Ink

A founder named Alexander Hamilton was George Washington's secretary, assistant, and adviser. He was the only person George Washington trusted to be in charge of spy operations, and he also wrote reports about how to improve the Continental army.

Alexander Hamilton was born on the island of Nevis, in the British West Indies. As an orphan, he struggled to make ends meet, but a group of people noticed his intelligence and sent him to America to get an education. He arrived in New York in 1773, when he was around sixteen years old. He soon rented a room in the home of a tailor named Hercules Mulligan, who convinced him to become a Patriot.

When Alexander Hamilton was about twenty-two years old, George Washington heard that he was a brilliant writer and thinker and offered him a job. Soon Alexander Hamilton knew the identities of spies, investigated double agents, and wrote and received messages in invisible ink! At first glance, the letters appeared to be about everyday life.

But between the lines, another message was hidden from sight! To read it, Alexander Hamilton dabbed the paper with a special chemical that made the "invisible" words appear on the page!

Alexander Hamilton also helped recruit a spy who saved George Washington's life! George Washington asked if he knew anyone who might be a trustworthy spy and was often around British soldiers. Hamilton immediately thought of his old friend Hercules Mulligan, who, in addition to being a tailor, ran a successful clothing shop. It had many British customers, including soldiers, whom he talked with while taking measurements for their clothes.

Hercules Mulligan agreed to be a spy and reported back to George Washington whenever he heard British secrets.

One cold winter night a British soldier rushed into the shop and said he needed a warm coat immediately. Hercules Mulligan asked why he was in such a hurry. The soldier said that he had to stand guard outside all night and that the British knew where George Washington was staying and planned to capture him! George Washington's life was in danger!

Hercules Mulligan tried to stay calm so the soldier wouldn't suspect anything. But as soon as the soldier left with his new coat, Hercules Mulligan sprang into action! He needed to warn Alexander Hamilton and George Washington, but couldn't risk taking the news to them himself. If the British spotted them together, they would know he was a spy! Instead, he sent a man he trusted to pass on the information.

It worked! George Washington got the
news in time. He was safe . . . and so was
Hercules Mulligan's secret!

Chapter 4
Secret Codes

In 1778, George Washington asked an army major named Benjamin Tallmadge to create a group of skilled secret agents to gather intelligence in British-occupied New York. It was so secretive that George Washington didn't even want to know the agents' real names!

The secret agents became known as the Culper Spy Ring, because they used variations of "Samuel Culper" as their code names. They were also known as the Secret Six, because there were six members: Robert Townsend, Abraham Woodhull, Austin Roe, James Rivington, Caleb Brewster, and Anna Strong.

Robert Townsend's code name was Samuel Culper Jr. He was a reporter who pretended to be a Tory so he could get intelligence for the Patriots.

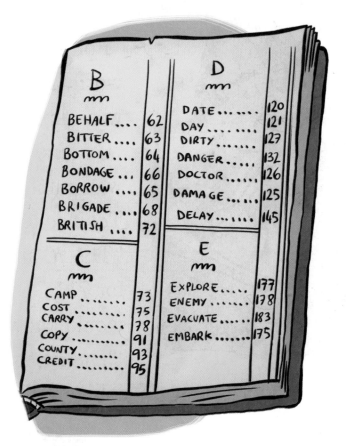

It was very dangerous, so Major Tallmadge created a secret code to help send information safely. Secret codes disguise messages by replacing words with different numbers or letters. Major Tallmadge assigned specific numbers to hundreds of different words and wrote them down in a giant codebook that he gave to the Culper Spy Ring members to help them write and decode messages.

For example, the word "British" was number 72. "General Washington" was number 711. If Townsend wrote, "The 72 are looking for 711!" the spies would know it meant "The British are looking for General Washington!"

Caleb Brewster was in charge of taking messages to and from George Washington, by sailing his boat across Long Island Sound. But the British knew he was a spy, so his location had to be kept secret or he could be captured.

Anna Strong lived on Long Island
Sound and could see his boat arrive from
her house. She came up with a clever way
to alert the Culper Spy Ring agents to the
boat's arrival without the British finding out.
She used her clothesline! When she hung

her black petticoat on the line, it signaled to the Culper Spy Ring that the boat was arriving. She also assigned a number to each of the nearby coves in Long Island Sound. She hung a specific number of white handkerchiefs on the clothesline to tell the agents where to meet to get the messages!

All these tactics helped George Washington lead the Continental army to victory in 1783, when Britain officially granted independence to the United States of America!

But spying didn't end there. Soon after, Thomas Jefferson became the US diplomat to France. When he found out his mail was being read, he invented a wheel cipher to help scramble his messages to keep them secret. A cipher disguises a message by mixing up the letters of each word with different letters or numbers, or by arranging them in a different order.

GHALMQT

I AM FINE

He had carved the alphabet onto the edges of twenty-six wooden discs that spun around a metal rod. He could spin the discs around until the letters spelled out what he wanted to say, and then look at the line above or below those words to find a row of *scrambled* letters to write in a note!

A reader could use an identical wheel cipher to decode the message in the note. For example, if Thomas Jefferson wrote "G HA LMQT," the reader would spin the discs around until the letters matched. Then the reader would look for a line above or below that was written in plain English and see that the message really said "I AM FINE"!

The founders were clever, brave, and dedicated, and those are just a few of the qualities that helped them spy their way to freedom!

One of the British officers who was defeated during the Revolutionary War said, "Washington did not really out-fight the British. He simply out-spied us."

There were also many unknown people who risked their lives to spy for a cause they believed in. Without them, the United States might still be a British colony!

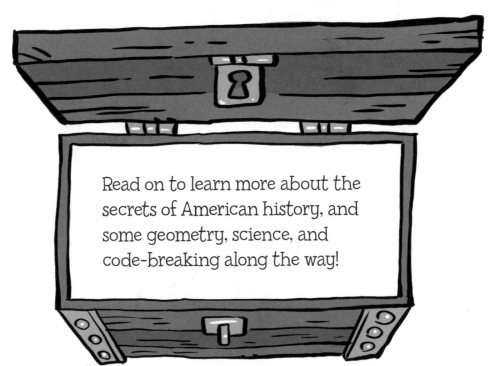

Read on to learn more about the secrets of American history, and some geometry, science, and code-breaking along the way!

Spy Some Symmetry!

The British spied on the Patriots too. They hid tiny rolled-up messages inside the hollow quills of feather pens, used mask letters, and more! A **mask letter** looks like a regular letter, but it can only be read with a piece of paper called a mask that has a hole cut in it. When the mask is placed on top of the letter, the border around the hole hides, or *masks*, the words in the letter that aren't important. The words that show through the hole in the mask are the true message!

This hourglass-shaped mask letter was sent by a British general. The shape of the mask is **symmetrical**! That means it can be divided in half along an invisible line called a **line of symmetry**. Both sides of the hourglass shape match, but they are mirror images.

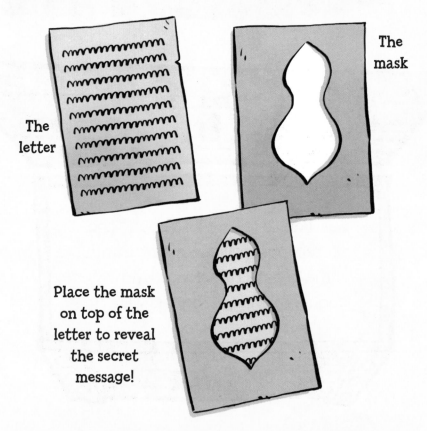

The letter

The mask

Place the mask on top of the letter to reveal the secret message!

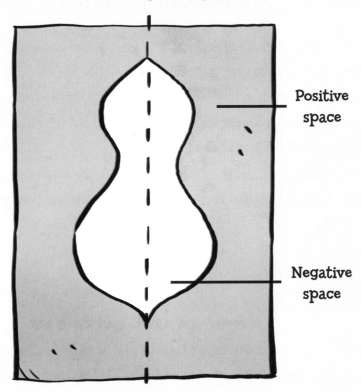

Line of symmetry

Positive space

Negative space

In this case, the line of symmetry is vertical, which means it runs from the top to the bottom of the hourglass shape. A line of symmetry can also be horizontal and go across a shape from side to side, or diagonal and go across a shape at an angle. Look around your world and see if you can find other shapes that are symmetrical!

This mask is also an example of positive and negative space. The paper is called **positive space** because it is an object. The space *around* the paper, including the hole in the middle, is called **negative space** or **background**. The edges of an object are what give shape to the negative space around it. Even though it's called positive and negative space, one kind isn't better or worse than the other.

All About Invisible Ink!

When you write a letter using a regular ink pen, the ink acts a bit like dye on the paper. **Invisible ink**, on the other hand, requires a chemical reaction to become visible. During the American Revolution, both sides used a kind of invisible ink that changed color when it was exposed to heat!

George Washington asked a friend to develop a *new* kind of invisible ink. Instead of using heat, he wanted ink that would only be visible after it was treated with a secret chemical. Soon he, Alexander Hamilton, and the Patriot spies used what they called the "sympathetic stain"!

Make Your Own Invisible Ink

Head to the grocery store to get ingredients to make your own invisible ink! All you need are baking soda, purple grape juice (from concentrate works best), and water . . . plus something to paint with. **Be sure to ask a grown-up to help you!**

1. Measure half a cup of baking soda and pour it into a small bowl.

2. Add half a cup of water (so you have equal parts baking soda and water).

3. Stir baking soda and water together.

4. Dip a cotton swab, toothpick, or paintbrush into the baking soda mixture and use it to write a secret message!

You will get the best results if you write on a plain white piece of paper. When the "ink" dries, it will be almost invisible!

When you're ready to reveal your secret message, ask a grown-up to pour you a cup of grape juice! Careful: Grape juice can stain your clothes or furniture!

Use a new cotton swab or toothpick, or a clean paintbrush, to paint the grape juice onto the paper. As the grape juice comes into contact with the baking soda, a chemical reaction takes place and your secret message will appear!

How It Works

Grape juice is an acid and baking soda is a base. Acids and bases are chemical opposites. When they are mixed together, the acid in the grape juice interacts with the base in baking soda, making it change color from white to a grayish purple.

Decode a Secret Message!

One code used by Major Tallmadge and the Culper Spy Ring replaced words with sets of numbers, and used a dictionary called *Entick's Dictionary* as a codebook. Each set of three numbers pointed to a page number, line number, and specific word of the codebook!

To write a message, he first looked in the dictionary to find a page that included a word he wanted to use. If he was using *this* book as a codebook to come up with a code for the word "decode," he could use 46.1.1. Here's how it works:

The first number points to the page number where the word can be found in the codebook. The first number in this code is 46, which means that you should turn to *page 46* of this book. That's *this* page!

The second number points to which line the word is on (including chapter titles like "Chapter 1" and section titles like "Decode a Secret Message!"). The second number in this code is 1, which means that the word is on the *first line* on this page.

The third number points to where the word is located on that line. The third number in this code is 1, which means the word is the *first word* on that line.

Decode This Secret Message Using *This* Book as a Codebook!

Check the answer section on the next page when you are ready. You can also use this code to write a message to a friend!

THE FOUNDING FATHERS WERE SPIES! QUIZ

1. What year was the Second Continental Congress?

a. 1774   b. 1775   c. 1789

2. What is another name for Tories?

a. Patriots   b. spies   c. Loyalists

3. What do you call someone who appears to be loyal to one country while secretly spying for another country?

a. double agent   b. secret spy   c. both a and b

4. What did Anna Strong use to send secret signals to the Culper Spy Ring?

a. dictionary   b. invisible ink   c. clothesline

5. Benjamin Franklin wrote secret letters to foreign leaders as part of which committee?

a. Secret Committee   b. Committee of Secret   c. Secret Messages
                              Correspondence   Committee

6. What did Alexander Hamilton use to write messages to George Washington's spies?

a. invisible ink   b. sympathetic stain   c. both a and b

7. What did a British soldier ask Hercules Mulligan to make that helped reveal a plot to capture George Washington?

a. boots   b. coat   c. wig

8. What kind of tool did Thomas Jefferson invent to write in code?

a. wheel cipher   b. wheel code   c. nothing

Answer to "Decode a Secret Message!" on the previous page: Decoded text reads "Send message to Washington!"

Answers: 1.b 2.c 3.a 4.c 5.b 6.c 7.b 8.a